Landlocked

Landlocked

POEMS BY **JULIA McCONNELL**

WHEELBARROW BOOKS ▪ *East Lansing, Michigan*

♾ The paper used in this publication meets the minimum requirements
of ANSI/NISO Z39.48-1992 (R 1997) (Permanence of Paper).

Wheelbarrow Books
Michigan State University Press
East Lansing, Michigan 48823-5245

LIBRARY OF CONGRESS CATALOGING-IN-PUBLICATION DATA
Names: McConnell, Julia, author.
Title: Landlocked : poems / by Julia McConnell.
Description: First. | East Lansing, Michigan : Wheelbarrow Books, [2023]
Identifiers: LCCN 2022043048 | ISBN 978-1-61186-457-1 (paperback) |
ISBN 978-1-60917-732-4 | ISBN 978-1-62895-498-2
Subjects: LCGFT: Poetry.
Classification: LCC PS3613.C38147 L36 2023 | DDC 811/.6—dc23
LC record available at https://lccn.loc.gov/2022043048

Cover design by Erin Kirk
Cover art: Adobe Stock | mykytivoandr

Visit Michigan State University Press at *www.msupress.org*

With the publication of Julia McConnell's *Landlocked*, the Residential College in the Arts and Humanities (RCAH) Center for Poetry at Michigan State University offers its twelfth book in our Wheelbarrow Books Poetry Series. Clearly, we pay homage to William Carlos Williams and his iconic poem, "The Red Wheelbarrow." Readers will remember the poem begins "so much depends upon . . ." that red wheelbarrow. In our country today with significant issues of climate change, inflation, COVID variants, cultural fracture, and political unrest, many people would say their lives do not depend upon poetry. Far from it. Ezra Pound told us that "poetry is news that stays news." This is not "fake news," or yesterday's news, or old news. Good poems have immediacy, present us with specific people in specific situations not unlike our own, and most of all, poems tell us the truth. "The first function of poetry is to tell the truth," June Jordan reminds us, "to learn how to do that, to find out what you really feel and what you really think."

Julia McConnell has her pen on the pulse of Oklahoma, on the pulse of love and longing, on the pulse of memory and metaphor. Here is the voice of a landlocked woman with a landlocked heart, living in a landlocked state (though I read recently that Nebraska is the most landlocked state in the country). Her love-hate relationship with her home and native state may remind many readers of why they left the places they were born and raised, why they want to go back, but why they can't. As a native West Virginian, I share many of McConnell's responses to the people and places of home, high mountains and tall trees replacing the wide, wide skies and prairie grasses, mining replacing the oil rigs, prejudices and politics problematic for us both. For many of us, no matter where we're from, we've outgrown home or left it behind. In "My Ex-Girlfriend, Oklahoma," McConnell writes,

> Dear Oklahoma,
> By the time you read this I'll be gone six months
> and you'll just be getting out of lock up
> for your second DUI.
> Listen, I'm sorry, but

> you are a bad girlfriend
> you keep breaking my heart
> and embarrassing me in public.

In these poems we see the sprawling open spaces of Oklahoma, but also the landlocked minds of religious and political conservatives from which this young lesbian librarian needs to break free. This librarian has read her books. Her poems invite in and pay homage to Elizabeth Bishop, Tennessee Williams, Walt Whitman, Mark Doty, Alicia Ostriker, and William Carlos Williams. She names friends and relatives, and we feel we've met them, too. Even her dog, Molly Marlova Magdalena McConnell, stars in a delightful poem. If you know a Jack Russell, you know this dog.

That's the thing about these poems. They'll sit with you in the living room like an old friend, or on your lap like an insistent pet, or you'll work alongside some employee folding shirts in a Dillard's Department Store, or run around in your swimsuit, drinking water from a backyard hose on a hot summer day. "Any small thing can save you," McConnell writes in "Scripture of the Fireflies," and "It is easy to miss these things." The poet is *saved,* one might say, by many small things in these poems: a photograph of her aunt when she worked on a detasseling crew in her youth; a painting by John Singer Sargent; "walking slow / through tall grass / indigo above / we are sky deep"; or lying "in the bed of a truck as the stars / unroll their holy blanket" in "this vast space of nothing / so full of something."

McConnell's portrait of Oklahoma is not one to be found in a tourist brochure, but it is endearing and enraging at the same time. She shows us the push-pull of what she loves and what she fears, her rich red-dirt past and a future she hopes to find just beyond the horizon. There is harshness and tenderness here, political commentary and personal vulnerability. She sees her home state as "a half feral cat / mewing at the back step." In "Tulsa 1998" she tells us

> Late summer evenings we'd drive
> down Riverside bouncing over
> bumps seeking mirages of
> glamor in that petroleum town
> its art deco ghosts, a stone
> church on every corner.

In a ghazal that's a meditation on the word *work*, she contemplates the botched execution of Clayton Lockett. Finally, in "How I Spent my Summer Vacation," McConnell writes, "Green all but gone by late summer back / home. Heat and humidity oppressive, / I longed for a suitcase of my own." Of this book she has made her suitcase, constructed it of "Books, Boots, and the Blank Page," packed it with elegies, love songs, postcards, Grandma Minnie's wedding band, and much more. With a nod to William Carlos Williams and to the truthfulness of poetry, in "Amuse-Bouche," Julia McConnell sings, "Who shall say I am not / the most beautiful woman in my town?"

As our number of Wheelbarrow Books increases, we hope that our audience increases also. Help us spread the word. In the beginning was the word, we're told, and the word became the poem. So much depends upon the collaboration of reader, writer, and poem, the intimate ways we come to know one another.

—ANITA SKEEN, *Wheelbarrow Books Series Editor*

Of the manuscripts I reviewed, while all had merit, I found *Landlocked* the most compelling and would most like to see it with the Wheelbarrow Books imprint on it. The poet's sense of place as central to both personal and public narrative strikes powerful chords with this reader, as do the diction, images, management of white space, and formal choices made in creating and assembling this powerful collection. Thank you for the opportunity to read this work in words and to welcome its maker into the standing army of essential, if neglected, poets.

—THOMAS LYNCH

In Memory of Karen Mayes

CONTENTS

Landlocked

Symptoms of Escape Fever Include

a dazzle sprouting from your chest
waltzing weeping vomiting
second-guess shoelaces winding around your larynx
microscopic bees zipping in your veins
queenly tours of red dirt wash

monarchs composing abdication speeches
constructing tinfoil hats to deflect guilt
empathy for meteors approaching black holes
permanent alteration while crossing event horizon

mudstone crumbling from your vision
trying out prodigal around the homeplace
tug of war between claustrophobic and agoraphobic
while traversing the plains by automobile

your home state a half feral cat
mewing at the back step
close the door
turn up the radio

Dillard's Department Store Field Guide

from *National Geographic Complete Birds of North America*, 2nd edition

How to straitjacket a dress shirt
back into its pins and plastic,
to roll jeans cuff to back pocket,
the different fit between Levi's
made in Sri Lanka and those from Lesotho.
How to fold T-shirts over a plexiglass rectangle
to pile merchandise in precise origami towers.
The art and practice of fieldcraft is a skill
that develops with time.

Breaks I smoke cigarettes, drink Diet Coke
in the shade of the loading dock
watch the crows across the street
wheel against late autumn blue
or pace through the fields, gleaning.
I take flight *with low, rowing wingbeats*
back to the salesfloor.

The make-up counter girls terrify
their blade sharp eyeliner
masks of foundation and powder
secrets of serums and salves.
Tyrant Flycatchers—graceful and beautiful
are also common and easy to observe.
Long afternoons digging
through the forgotten back stock
they sniff the old man colognes.

I study at lunch in the food court
where a group of sparrows live
foraging for French fries
and Chick-fil-A nuggets.

A sparrow with only one mangled leg
scoots across the tiled floor
between the metal chairs.
The proportions of its wings
and tail are unremarkable.

To rule over men's
accessories and all the tiny hooks,
the dozens of variations of black dress socks
the packages of jockey shorts, briefs,
and boxers, *plumage—a dull collection of brown, gray,*
black, and white, Marvel, with all the best gossip,
drives forty miles from Chandler.
Frequently misidentified as a sweet old lady,
until you hear her foul mouth,
or get drunk off her bourbon
balls at Christmas.

Tornado season, staff and customers take shelter
in the basement furniture department,
to sit shoulder to shoulder on sectionals
in front of the big screens and watch
the dryline, hook echo, supercells.
The nest—a loose platform of twigs, flimsy.

Outside the parking garage
a mourning dove dead on the sidewalk
its wings spread wide, feet in the air,
creamy grey feathers,
blush like a fallen blossom
tiny black marble eye.

Coming Out in Oklahoma

after Audre Lorde

I'm supposed to say
I think Brad or Jason
is hot
that I want to lick his abs
have his babies
make him a sandwich.
But I never really got it
until that one night
she pulled me into a bathroom
to show me a mirror
and kissed me hard.
Then I got it.

Elizabeth Bishop Swipes Right

after Elizabeth Bishop's "Arrival at Santos"

Here is a bar; here is a Wendy's;
here, after an endless diet of horizon, a parking lot;
asphalt cracked and buckling and—well, shit—the narrow spaces
are all taken outside the unmarked building,

with the heavy steel door. Across the street
by the real estate office, is where you should park
so your windows won't be bashed. *Oh, tourist,*
is this how this country is going to answer you

and your immodest demands for a different world,
and a better life, and complete satisfaction
of love at last, and immediately,
after twenty-four years of denial?

Get out your ID. Friendly is waiting,
the gruff butch behind the glass, writing down your name,
before buzzing you in to a cloud of cigarette smoke
and country music. This is still Oklahoma,

of course, not unlike any other bar in this town.
And football on TV, even some crosses on necks
as we make our thirsty way to the long line at the bar,
myself, and fellow lonely heart, Miss Bishop

navigating through the chaos of women spinning
in each other's arms across the dance floor
while Brooks and Dunn wail about Lorca's neon moon.
Oh, Miss Bishop! This is not the kind of joint

where you order wine. How 'bout a beer
or whiskey? Or a shot of tequila? Here comes Dezi,

she's just shaved her head, home from deployment.
Let's grab that table while we can.

There. We are settled. Listen, not
a lot of strangers here, so if they don't know
you, they're not likely to talk to you. It takes a while.
Buy some drinks, share your smokes, soon

you'll be a regular, or on the next bus out of town.
Do you wanna two-step? Throw some darts?
Or just sit back, watch the show, and chain smoke until
last call at 2 a.m.? We'll call you a taxi, ha! Just kidding,

no taxis here. We'll walk you to your car,
drive behind you, or tell you to text us when you get home
safe, but never let you walk into the parking lot alone.
We are drilled into the interior.

Tennessee Williams Speaks to Joe Exotic about the Southern Gothic

A found poem sourced from *Cat on a Tin Roof*

Big Daddy, Big Money
King of the Misfits,
When the world tried to make you small
shameful and filthy
you just got bigger.
All your life like a doubled-up fist
pounding, smashing, driving
off bridges or into the city
to find yourself a boy
tossing condoms at the pride parade
selling steak sauce, sex gel, and underwear
in the end *your dixie stars never made a nickel.*

Everybody keeps hollering about the truth
the truth is as dirty as lies.
We occupy the same cage, you and I,
Southern and queer.
Our daddies hated us.
We tried to forge our own families.
And now look at you
nothin' and nobody except big daddy yourself.

What are you running away from?
There are simply things in this world
you gotta face, baby
avarice, greed, mendacity
when the one you love doesn't love you.
The truth is dreams don't come true.

What is the victory of a tiger
on a corrugated aluminum roof?

To stay on as long as he can.
Now the roof is cracking.
Tornados are headed for the zoo.
A cage is no kind of shelter.

Work: A Ghazal for Oklahoma

State Motto: *Labor Conquers All Things*

I learned about the battle over the lethal drugs
on the radio while driving home from work.

There are thick reference books on pharmaceuticals
and slim volumes on death at the library where I work.

I know women in Oklahoma who wear a uniform
and make prisoners stand behind a line for their work.

There are lawyers who defend murderers and rapists
and try to keep them from the execution chamber for their work.

I try not to drink too much wine after a day contending
with screaming toddlers and grumpy customers at work.

Twelve journalists watched Lockett struggle from the gurney
moaning. To be witnesses is their work.

News of the botched execution scrolled onscreen while I watched
The Voice, where the singers, uninterrupted, performed their work.

It is unethical for doctors to execute, so prison workers
administered the drugs, unqualified for such work.

I was taught in Sunday school, it is a Beatitude
to visit prisoners. This is a saint's work.

Sometimes I watch *Law and Order*
to see justice at work.

After his vein collapsed, after the viewing window was closed,
forty-three minutes after his first injection, Lockett's heart stopped its work.

Clayton Lockett shot Stephanie Neiman
and buried her alive. This is evil's work.

Stephanie's parents live
with their grief. This is their work.

Compounding pharmacies mix drugs that Europe
won't sell to us. We pay them for their work.

The next morning I lie in bed and listen to the news.
I know we are all complicit in this work.

Foreman of the Detasseling Crew

She sits in the cutter's high seat,
turned away from the machine's wheel
her muscled forearms tanned
dark against the rolled-up sleeves
of her men's white shirt, buttoned
at the collar. Men's blue jeans, too,
cuffed over her heavy leather boots.
Her hand rests on her knee
a cigarette between her fingers.
It is the end of day.

The photographer on the ground
one of her sisters,
most likely, in this all-girl
detasseling crew
points the camera
so that she is framed
against the freedom
of the wide sky.

In just this moment after pulling
the break, killing the engine,
and lighting up, she shares
a laugh while staring into
the middle distance.

She's earned it, this little
bit of peace having completed
a long day of men's labor
the fields of corn
a satisfying tally.

For just a few minutes more
before it's time to move

on home and cook supper
she is no one's wife
no one's daughter or mother
she is simply Helen
finishing her cigarette.

As Much for Worship as Entertainment

"In Deep Red Oklahoma, The Blue Door Is 'a Lighthouse'
for Progressive Protest Music," NPR, January 21, 2020

A neighborhood of patchy lawns, shambling porches,
rocky dirt parking in the empty lot
next door. No sign just blue double doors in
a square fieldstone building. Lobby papered
with tattered show posters. A dark room with
one hundred folding chairs, small stage cluttered
with instrument stands and cords. On the wall
Woody Guthrie points the way to glory,
Route 66 sign, Red 46 flag,
old banjo, tarnished trumpet. No room for
dancing. Beer bottles clink the concrete floor.
All you fascists bound to lose fills every
bone. Outside cicadas echo. The night air
is thick, holds the day's heat. Everything sweats.

Tulsa 1998

Freedom was learning to work
the clutch on the Volkswagen whose
glove box smelled like gasoline.
Late summer evenings we'd drive
down Riverside bouncing over
bumps seeking mirages of
glamor in that petroleum town
its art deco ghosts, a stone
church on every corner.

We were learning to dance.
We had nowhere for dancing.

I didn't want boys, but
wanted romance. What did I
imagine romance to be?
Distant music drifting like
smoke? A certain slant of light?
Lipstick, whiskey, somewhere else?

We had all just read *Gatsby*
so we played twilight croquet.
None of us seemed sure of rules.
Restless with genteel tapping
we began swinging mallets
like golf clubs, launching balls
skyward, oblivious to
park perambulators prey
to our falling projectiles.

Outside the abandoned train
depot we took turns at the
center of the universe
a small circle of concrete
an acoustical vortex
screaming to hear our echo.

The Next-to-Last Lesbian Bar in Oklahoma City

Sisters was the only girl's
bar on the strip, a street
the older drag queens warned us
never walk alone at night.
By day it stood abandoned,

gray concrete buildings, blacked out
windows, next to the cross town
highway, ramshackle apartments
behind chain-link fences.
The night hid those things.

All the girls smoked Marlboro
Reds, drank Bud Light, carried men's
billfolds, revolved between bar,
dance floor, pool tables, and darts.
No men's room, just a single

with a sign: *one at a time.*
We hollered conversations
over the DJ's music;
Loosen up my buttons babe;
then: *Here's your one chance Fancy*

don't let me down. Sherry, blind
in one eye, taught me to two-
step, physics of pivot turns,
how to place my thigh between
her thighs, to press my pelvis

forward, lean back, and follow.
When single, I wanted a
girlfriend. When taken, I wanted
to flirt with the bartender
with glasses and a braid.

She called me Trouble, but smiled
for the women's football studs
who sold dollar Jell-O shots.
Sisters closed when Deb wanted
to retire. None of us girls

had money to buy the place.
Too soon it became Phoenix
Rising, a men's leather bar,
where I got kicked out at Pride
for skipping the long lines and

peeing in the (now) men's room
insisting it was still our bar.
The next morning when I picked
up my car, I found the tags
cut off the plates with shears.

The Land We Belong To

Oklahoma needs to lose some weight
    is gonna go back to school someday
    giggles when the earth shakes.

Oklahoma sits on the porch drinking a beer
    watching the storm roll in
    helps her neighbor clean up after the tornado.

Oklahoma carries a big purse
    marries a guy name Brad
    drives a SUV.

Oklahoma comes home dirty from the oil fields
    gets a check from the wind farms
    has a job but needs another to pay the bills.

Oklahoma wants to sing like cicadas
    on hot summer nights
    how the horizon feels like longing.

Oklahoma got pregnant at fifteen
    wants to know when you are getting married
    invites you to church on Sunday.

Oklahoma is a good guy with a gun
    steals your land
    locks up your momma.

Oklahoma wants to tell you about her home
    dirt the color of blood
    sunsets better than Saturday night.

Oklahoma prays for you
    your unborn baby
    and oil.

Oklahoma waits for rain.

Graciela Says

after "Ojos Para Volar"

If you fell madly in love
would you stay
in your imagined country?

Exist in the in-between
enter a world unknown
unclipped word wings
moving inside, aware
of the many angles of truth.

Learn to use your bird sight.
Become bird
be filled with birds.
Plant birds in the earth
grow eyes to fly with.

Call out to a bird
bigger than yourself
words falling from your lips.
Feed the aviary that lives inside.
The birds are singing to you
trust this song.
Open the wings behind your eyes—
see the fragments
always in midflight.

Damnation Isn't a Bad Word Cuz They Say It in Church

The kids at school say that the world's gonna end on Saturday.
And I was like, *Nuh-uh, the world can't end.*
And they said, *Yeah uh-huh it can.*
The preacher on the radio said it would.
God's gonna beam up all the good holy people to heaven
in the middle of whatever they're doin'.
You could be playing soccer or watching TV
or whatever and suddenly God's gonna pick you up
and you're gonna fly up to Jesus.

The kids at school say that on Saturday
when all the good church-going people fly up to heaven
there is gonna be a big earthquake
that's gonna destroy the whole world.
All the sinners will be left to suffer eternal damnation.

I told them they shouldn't say damn,
that's a bad word.
But they said it was okay
because damnation is not the same as damn
and besides the preacher said it in church
which makes it okay.

I asked them if dogs
have to wear leashes in Heaven
cuz my dog Meatball is a real good dog
but he don't like leashes.
They said dogs don't get to come to heaven
cuz they don't have souls.
I said that Meatball does too have a soul.
I'm not gonna go to Heaven
if he can't come too.

The kids at school say
that I don't get to go to heaven,
that I have to stay on earth
and suffer eternal damnation
since my family don't go to church.

So I asked my mom
what eternal damnation was
when she picked me up from school
and she said, *What?*
And I said, *Eternal Damnation, what's that?*
She wanted to know where I heard that.
I asked her why we didn't go to church.
She said, *Well they used to go to church*
when they were kids like me
but now they don't believe in all that stuff.
And I said can we please please please go to church
cuz I'm scared that Meatball or me or grandma
is gonna fall in the giant crack in the ground and die.

She wanted to know what on earth
I was talking about.
I told her what the kids at school say.
She said I should pay them no mind
that the preacher on the radio is a crazy person.

I guess she's probably right
since my other mom said the same thing.
But after dinner Meatball and I were playing outside
I looked up and there was this great big cloud in the sky.
It was pink and gold and orange.
It looked like the Starship Enterprise.
So I went and got my binoculars
to see if I could see Jesus
up there in the clouds.
I wanted to talk to him

because maybe he would let me and Meatball
come to heaven anyway.
But I couldn't see him
and Mom said it was time
to go to bed.

Slip 'N Slide

Someone tells you
water has no taste
but they've never drunk
from a backyard hose
on a hot summer's day.

That metallic almost dirty
almost good taste
with a little bit of green
from the freshly cut grass.

You're in your swimsuit.
running around
with the kids across the street
launching
down the yellow plastic sheeting
slick with water
skin carpet-burning
when you hit a dry spot.

You are tired.
You are hungry.
You don't want this to end.
Grownups are telling you
it's time.

Time to put your clothes back on.
Time for dinner.
Time for church.
Time because
they've simply had enough.

Drunk on sun and laughing
you begin to cry.
The taste of water
running down your face—
salty and sweet.

How I Spent My Summer Vacation

after John Singer Sargent's *Carnation, Lily, Lily, Rose*

Always I wanted to live in the painting
brightening the wall of my mother's sewing
closet, cut from a calendar: two girls
deep in Midsummer, lighting lanterns at
evening's twilight in an emerald garden
flush with stargazers and roses.

Green all but gone by late summer back
home. Heat and humidity oppressive,
I longed for a suitcase of my own.

July is a time for traveling. Even butterflies
know it's time to rise above the tree line and
live off your caterpillar fat.

Mr. Sargent spent two years painting his masterpiece.
Near twilight he set up his easel to wait for the
opulence of mauve-ish dusk,
painting for twenty minutes or two, as long as the
quality of light would last. As autumn came, he
replaced the dying flowers with artificial blossoms,
switched his models for girls more suitable.

Time crawled in the harsh light of three o'clock when I
unfurled my summers in my room
vanishing into stories. For birthdays
we drove to vacant lots to cut
xeriscape bouquets of sunflowers and thistles, a still life amid
yards of Bermuda grass and sprinklers,
zinnias that kept growing back no matter the cuttings.

An Education

I was a good student, all the history textbooks
I read were unmarked graves in Tulsa.

In fourth grade I memorized the names of the five friendly tribes
whose death march landed them in Tulsa.

In high school the correct answer on the test:
The civil war was fought over states' rights, not slavery in Tulsa.

Sometimes I'd go swing dancing at the VFW
where they'd sing *Livin' in the Time of Tulsa*.

Natalie Merchant played the Brady Theater (named after a Klansman)
she said we had a lot of churches in Tulsa.

Oral Roberts built a harvest gold campus of spaceships
to get closer to God in Tulsa.

Carlton Pearson, lost his church, Higher Dimensions
when he declared there was no hell in Tulsa.

All us south side Socs loved *The Outsiders*
about poor kids fighting rich kids in Tulsa.

When I learned about the massacre it was called a riot.
I was told a black man started it in Tulsa.

Oil rigs dig deep for justice, for God,
cover up the bodies buried shallow in Tulsa.

Grandma Minnie's Wedding Band

Once we were both newly minted
untarnished, fresh out of the press
of high school. A graduated gal
with newly sheared bob
caught the hired hand's eye.
When he placed me on her finger
I made the girl a wife
and bound us to our labor.

Two hundred forty acres of corn and soy. Fifteen baby
heads to cradle and naughty limbs to smack.
Thirteen ducklings always following. Two boys,
twins, to place in the ground
that winter no one could stay warm.
One husband, too many bottles to hide.
No time for the books she loved.

His hands were too big to turn the breached piglet,
so we made that warm and bloody journey.
Baloney and beans every day.
Hogs were for selling, not for eating.
But string beans, snap peas, tomatoes
body warm on the vine, were for the table
tended in soil that caught in my circumference.

At the end her fingers were so swollen
I almost went in the ground too.

Now I sit untouched in the jewelry box.
Little girl hands graze the broaches
the bracelets and the red bead rosary.
A simple white gold band thin
enough to be mistaken for a washer.

Boundless

When I drive west on I-40
through the ochre oceans
of plains just past Amarillo
I want to stop the car and walk
toward horizon
no destination but alone
in the big empty
the tall grass brushing
against my legs
wind filling my ears
sun hot on my neck
promising
to go at least as far
as the next boundary
between earth and sky.

I watch mockingbirds swoop
and dive, white stripes flashing
and wonder if they feel fear
while flying. I try to place myself
inside their tiny bodies
my heart pumps faster
wind rushing under wings
soaring through the empty sky
held aloft in nothing.

I want to drive
out to nowhere and lie down
in the bed of a truck as the stars
unroll their holy blanket
surrender myself to the terror
of this vast space of nothing
so full of something.

Elizabeth Bishop Reads My Horoscope

First things first,
move to Brazil.
No, that's second.
First get on a boat.

Tell yourself you are going on vacation.
Taste guava, cashew, mango, papaya.
The first act is to delude yourself.
Hope is a firefly constantly going out

and lighting up again. I never
mastered the art of postcards always
too many words to fit in one square.
I never wanted to drop it in the box

to surrender my words. My life—
one small postcard I kept
trying to rewrite while
drinking from a fountain of gin.

I never lost the right things.
Continents vanished,
but never my thirst.
Poems vanished

between the keys of my typewriter.
Losing, an art you can't help but paint,
absence always in the spotlight.
Maybe I should have sent those postcards

addressed but blank
desire's empty promises.
One day the mail just stops
return to sender.

Swallow another drink
or better yet, spit it out.
I made my escape through the bottle's
small neck but never managed to get out.

My miracles were burning
balloons falling from the sky
small animals fleeing
alone into black night

the way lips find each other in the dark.
Or these words to your mouth.
Handwritten postcards yellow
hidden in a shoebox.

Better to write poems
even if you wrestle
the ending
for years.

At the Public Library

Once petal pink
now with a patina of sticky fingers
graham crackers and playground
this floppy bunny
fur loved off in patches
found in the parking lot.

Nearby in a backdoor alcove
the nest we watched
with four blue eggs
then three squirming blind open mouths
then two sets of not-quite-ready wings
is gone.

34

Notes on Sky-Watching

Today the sky is a scattering of pebbles,
a fragment of pelvic bone
found in the desert,
a hedgehog,
a schooner,
a tanker.

Today there are four people
I want to call,
two of whom are dead.

Today cerulean.
somber steel,
bruise purple,
storm current
as the sky bares its hundreds of mammatus clouds
before tearing itself open with rain.

Today the sky seems light
but I am told that each cumulus
cloud is the weight
of a hundred elephants.
You could feel like drowning
standing on the plains looking up.

Turkey vulture, raptor, mockingbird.
Today locusts sing the ticking clockwork of the sky.

Today I can't call the sky
or a hotline to speak with the dead.
It hurts to look at sky without sunglasses.

I forget to look at the sky
and what would I say anyway?

Today the sky lights up over small-town traffic
refracting atmospheric particles into crimson organdy.
It's not words I want to hear but a voice.

The sky is silent.
The wind hardly whispers.

Today there are four people
I want to call
two of whom are dead.

Blue Surprise

I've never seen an August
this green
it's in the way the dark
and the light
keep moving
I can't stop touching it
and between us
a new kind of bird
mourning dove
Mississippi kite
crow song
oil derricks wanton
on the horizon
walking slow
through tall grass
indigo above
we are sky deep

Last Day of 37

Maybe it is good
      to move out of a prime
number
      into something divisible
to let go
      to fall apart
          and reassemble
to sweep up the dust
      of this last year
          and throw it away.
Everywhere the snow is melting
      exhalation of the old.
Better to count the years
      than to count what's left
better to bruise
      than to shatter
to give voice
      to the lyric unraveling
      startled snapshot
      radiant feast.

June Valentine

My heart sings the grackle's song
not pretty
but insistent
always hungry
picking tiny raspberry fools
out of brambles.

It is June
already summer berries grunt
daylilies begin their orange buckle
the season hobnobbing with decay.

Sirenita,
sunlight is untouchable
but it touches you
your skin, your hair
a tincture of flame.

I thought I would be there by now
in the treacle sponge
of green
you call home.
My heart a rhubarb mess
dropped on the pavement
ants licking the sweet syrup.

The solstice approaches.
Every day we are given
more light.
Every day I try
to stay awake.
Every day I hear you
humming
elsewhere

you the blue robin's egg
I carry in my pocket.

You say you are too old.
I say summer is short
long as firework's flare
a shiver of light
blooming and dissolving
against night's endless sky.
On the ground
faces lift
with pleasure.

Scripture of the Fireflies

after Mark Doty

The fireflies are trying to teach me
their besotted evening ceremony
pulse blink pulse blink
coy in the tall grass
revealing their instruments
to the wrens,
to the weeping raspberries.

I am locked in my tantrum
of longing and unbelonging
clutching at constellations
unwilling to accept the imperfect.
My back turned, blindfolded,
two swords in my hands.
I am sweeping mud.

It is time to stop looking away
at the phantom place
neck deep in shadow.

Any small thing can save you—
the whir of trumpeting crows,
a vine winding its way up,
birds taking flight
struck into a conflation of joy,
clearing your throat while singing
at dawn or twilight,
rendering words from cloud bank
about to break into rain.

It is easy to miss these things.

What is your leap limit?
Have you tested
the winking shimmer
of season's change?
Stasis is a lie.

A firefly lands on my belly
floats away.

Amuse-Bouche

after William Carlos Williams

If I when everyone else is going to church
or meeting friends for eggs and mimosas
and the sky is an ocean
roiling and angry
above grass that needs to be cut
if I in my kitchen
cook food and lots of it
and share only with my little dog
and sing softly to myself
"I am so in love
so in love
I was born to be in love
and never alone"
If I taste everything I cook
and grow plump
with squeezable breasts
and a double chin

Who shall say I am not
the most beautiful woman in my town?

Postcards

Mi Amor
you are the long extension cord of my heart
you, both *heimweh* and *fernweh*
are the knowledge I have not yet discovered
the far-off location of my homeland.

Querida
you are the existential panic
that comes after eating too much pizza
and drinking too much box rosé
and you, its antidote.

Corazón
remember Johnny B?
All he wanted
was to be a patriarch
or to have his own
instead he built labyrinths
repaired old clocks.

Mi Sirenita
Mi Pollita
it's another long night
at the lonely rodeo.
I wonder which bull you are riding.
Hasta la vista, baby.

Sunday Morning Elegy for Karen

Church people are lining up together
for eggs and pancakes
while I sit in a booth
sunburned and hungover
taking up space in this diner.
I want to call you so bad
it's an ache in a phantom chest
a phantom heart.

Keeper of my story, my secrets,
my sorrow, dead since January
every week you met me
at your office door
standing so tall, so slender.
You kept watch over me
with the beacon of your voice.
Even when I carried
razor blades in my pocket
you kept me safe.

Back at home I lie down on my couch.
You are sitting behind me in your chair.
There's the UPC sticker
still stuck to the ceiling tile
the painting of the water lilies
warm lamps lighting the dark room.
As usual we sit in silence until you speak:
Just say whatever comes to mind.
I know then that this will be
one of those sessions
where I crumple
wordless, overcome.
I hear your voice: *I know. I know.*

Books, Boots, and the Blank Page

after Alicia Ostriker

We've been dumped unceremoniously
into library's book drop
pages splayed, crumpled, exposed
left on airplanes in the pouch next
to the emergency safety instructions
stained by coffee, spaghetti, wine.
illustrated in crayon
by an unattended kindergartener
or left out in the rain.
Worse yet, stranded
on a dusty shelf overlooked.
All we want is to be held
to have our pages turned
to hold your gaze.

Take us with you say the boots
lined up against the bedroom wall.
Take us through your red dirt path
spring puddles, yellowed grass,
dog shit, it doesn't matter.
We want to travel.
Let us give weight to your swagger
a heavy heel that makes each hip
rise and swing as we step,
step, step, against the earth.
Everyone will hear you coming.
With a walk like that how
will anyone know
you are afraid?

Come to me says the blank page.
I'm the lover you can't believe
wants you.
In front of me you blush
look away, arms crossed.
You don't feel pretty enough.
But here I am
laid out in front of you
waiting.
Whisper secrets in my ears.
Trace your name on my shoulder.
Make me rise to your touch.

Another Poem about the Wind

When did the wind first tell you
the name it gave you—
tiny notes of music,
wild impermanence?
Let your bones make music.

About the Chicken

Saturday evening I call my mom
to ask if she thought the chicken
I've had in the fridge since Sunday
was worth freezing
or if I should throw it out.

Before I know it mom is crying
on the other end of the line saying
You fall in love so easy.

I am as flummoxed by this
as I am by the accumulated
minutiae of daily life—bits
of paper, old birthday cards,
funeral programs, keys
without a lock—wondering
if they are worth holding

on to, or my jealousy over
friends' happiness.
It is spring again. Everyone
is in love like in all of the old songs.
I am humming Gershwin, *A lucky*
star's above but not . . .

I've realized that thing
about mortality
it's no joke. Not just for me
but even the person I want to call
whose voice makes me feel
better. Now the best I can do is listen
to voice mails saved on my phone.

I get up and clean out the fridge
and there's that chicken
I don't know what to do with.

There are things that seem unbearable
I say sitting
on the porch drinking a beer,
dog on my lap.
But really, Mom,
I was just calling about
the chicken.

Molly Marlova Magdalena McConnell

My dog is not a metaphor.
She's too busy bunny-hopping through shrubbery
to bother with literary devices.

She has way more friends than me and gets more dates.

When we go for walks I love to watch her trot
on her stubby little legs, butt wiggling,
her tail, a tiny exclamation point.
When I lie down on the couch, hot and exhausted,
she stands on my chest, open mouthed,
and breathes her doggy breath in my face.

Molly sees with her nose and tastes with her eyes.
"Oh, shit! Squirrel tartare! Rawrf, Rawrf! Arruu, rahru
arwww, uuuu, oooo. Yawp!"
Molly is Walt Whitman when it comes to squirrels.
Other times she is a yogi, lying on my bed
feet in the air, demonstrating relaxation techniques.
She calls this one "Dead Cockroach."

She is not, exactly, a good dog.
She pulls on her leash, dragging me behind her.
She barks and snarls at other dogs. She doesn't like
other girls to make out with me, and will
get in between. She brings home ticks.
Mom once called Molly an ass-wipe
and then apologized to her later.

On lonely Saturday nights
Molly will put on her human costume
and come with me to the movies.
She is a tall, long-legged blond
with a mane of curly hair.

She sits in everyone's laps,
licks up spilled soda, eats popcorn off the floor.
When I scold her she says,
"Girl, you gotta get while the gettin's good.
Plus, this is the best floor ever!"

I go home with her anyways.
See? It's just like they say.
If you allow gay marriage,
librarians will marry
their Jack Russel Terriers.

She is the furry weight always next to me.
She is the white hair on my black clothes.
I pet her wiry coat the way monks touch prayer beads.
At night she sleeps on my pillow, snoring softly.
Fierce little beast of solace.

Second Sight Speaks

Up until last week I used to race cars in Monaco
a bona fide Formula One racer addicted
to the cocktail of g-force, adrenaline
and nearly crashing in fiery death
while taking a tight curve accelerating
along a mountain highway and feeling
the car lean over the edge
into the canyon below.

But I've given all of that up
for a lucrative career in fortune telling.
The second sight arrived in the mail
after I accumulated the requisite number
of blows to the head.

I've read your cards: all swords and towers.
Your palm is like a recipe.
I'm experimenting with crystal balls
of varying size and clarity
divination from tea leaves and apple cores
teeth marks on spare ribs nibbled neat.

I am pioneering a new technique
you jump out a plane
and by the trajectory of your fall
I can see your fate:
you never leave
you do not see the stars
you do not get lost
you never jump
your parachute never opens
you only have few moments left
before you hit the earth.

Long Lost

My therapist is at a truck stop.
She is stuck.
She lives there now
somewhere between home
and Ghost Ranch.
This explains why I keep coming back
to this particular roadside attraction.
This explains my fascination
with empty Amarillo, Texas.

How have I never seen her here before?
She's been here all this time
selling cigarettes and breakfast sandwiches
to weary travelers
cleaning the glass doors
the cases of colorful beer and energy drinks.

My therapist doesn't talk anymore.
She can only listen.
She gives directions—
Keep going.
Turn around.
Take this exit.
Slow down.
What she always doesn't say anymore:
dream on it for a while.

My therapist loves the ocean
but she is stranded
where the high plains
become the desert.
I live where it is wet and green.
I forget to visit the ocean.
I forget to see the mountains

shrouded in clouds.
I forget and see her in crowds.

My therapist doesn't answer
the phone anymore.
It just rings and rings.
I forget and think of things
I want to tell her—
I love you.
Goodbye.

My therapist works at a dusty truck stop
on the side of this long highway
where travelers can stop
to take comfort
from what the dead
might say
to the living.

Highway

I've started driving city streets instead.
I've started walking around my car
checking all the tires.
I've started staying always in the right lane
below the speed limit
resisting the temptation to pull off on the shoulder.

I am afraid of what is inside me.
Ever since that gray cloud
showed up in my left eye
and spread until I couldn't see.
Ever since discovering
those white smears on the MRI
the result of my body's friendly fire
T-cells chewing on myelin.
Ever since beginning treatment
a box of needles hiding in my fridge.

Hide in a bottle of wine
alone in your apartment
fearless dog on your lap.
Hide the brochures
in the back of your closet.
Hide yourself behind work
extra hours at the office
stomping around in your boss-lady boots
the woman with all the answers.
Hide from the Turner Turnpike
just don't go to Tulsa.
Hide in science or in silence.

Know
the slower you drive
the faster the big black truck
will catch up to you
ride your tail.
You are late already.

Love Song

I am the breath that begins your life
      and the breath that will end it.
I am the music knocking
      against the tiny bones of your ear
      the water entering you.
I am your nerves writing letters to your brain
      your eyes translating light
      the acid in your stomach
      that burns to the touch
      the heart that pumps your blood
      and the plaque that will stop it.
I am the silent lump in your left breast
      the needle piercing knowledge
      the mouth that kisses
      and longs to be kissed.
I am all the small things your body does
      without you knowing
      T-cells devouring myelin
      the dirt between your toes
      the wax in your ears
      the sneeze that baptizes your desk.
I am the skeleton pulling the strings
      the orgasm and the excrement
      the open arms of the earth
      waiting to welcome you.
I am the cries of the pig you are eating
      the fingernail clippings left in the grass
      the continent of plastic bags
      floating in the ocean.
I am all the worms.

Someday you'll love your body
  when you know it can fail.
Someday you'll kiss your skin
  the way I kiss yours.
Someday love
  will be no wine at all.
Someday the sun will go to sleep
  and we will be scattered to the four winds.
Someday I'll be inside your body.
  Until then, my dear.

Pulling Runes

The small white stone asks you
what beckons?
What wants to be known?
A ring around the full moon
the wind's inconsolable song
these are songs speaking to you
not to you
to no one at all.
Still there are doves
cooing in the trees
slugs eating apricots
ice particles refracting
dispersions of light.
Take an elevator to your heart
pass through the door
you never thought it possible
to be born.

Valentines 2018

All animals want to be loved
the goat in its pajamas
the cow with its head
in the farmer's lap
the skeletal polar bear
wandering in a land without ice
even my fat heart
on a diet for too long
caught between spinster
and odalisque.

While madmen rule the world
fingering annihilation's button
huffing dinosaur goo
deporting all dreamers
why are you so far away?

Listen, still there is music.
Saturday night I think of you
harmonies sweet as spring
band ablaze.
Why aren't we dancing?

Listen, there are horses
treading water
in a river of tears
come close
dance with me now.
We are just animals.

January 8, Yelapa, Mexico

I.
In the jungle your feet are always dirty
the night is never silent
dense with cries and crowing
shuffles and sighs
we can't remember how we got here
or why
we sit at the top of a dry waterfall
and weep for once was
twilight we bend our bodies
toward restoration
hold hands to heart center, third eye
breathe through it.
Unlike my teacher I cannot name
the muscle, the tendon, the chakra
for what is troubling me.
The night is very dark.
There are no doors.

II.
The ocean brings countless messages
relentless unceasing
I do not wade too deep
fearful of the undertow
sand slipping underneath my feet
go out far enough and the ocean
resembles the plains.
I am a landlocked woman.
January 8 rolls in every year
like the tide
like an unopened letter.

III.
It is moonlight
this anniversary of your death
and my birth
bright enough in the dark
no flashlight is needed
the blue glow keeps me up
comes through the door
to my jungle bed
forms shapes and shadows
on the wood floor
cheeks pressed together
birth and death dancing
in each other's arms
sweat mingling
breath mixing to the same song
the primordial mystery
that happens every day.
Listen very carefully now
for the next step in time:
quick quick slow.

In the New Year

Food will never go bad
in my fridge
junk mail will turn to love letters
and my heart
like some simple creature
(say a worm, for example)
will regenerate
each fragmented piece
becoming whole.
I will have at least five hearts
in my chest.

Keeping all five hearts
open at once
will be dangerously exhilarating
operating beyond capacity
a vehicle full throttle.
I will be lightning rod
and sponge
stone and sand
transmitter and receiver.
A heart to love the world
a heart to grieve it
another heart for falling in love
one for breaking
secret hearts tucked away
no one can ever touch.
When one heart is too full
it can close
while a dormant heart blooms
like eyes blinking open and shut
on the wings
of some terrible angel.
One heart to be scared
one heart to be brave.

I will have enough hearts to give away.
When I see you
I will simply reach
beneath the warm animal of my breast
between the hard bars of my ribs
and pluck a heart out
place it in your cupped hands
slick with blood, 98 degrees, still pumping.
I can always grow more.

On Why You Should Change Your Life Every Seven Years

Your skin will be different
but your bones will remain the same.

Belonging is a maze
you are not meant to escape.

Home is where you push
your body against the door to get it open.

We all have a fear of falling,
why not build a ladder to face it?

As a child you confused the words sacred and scared.
You still do sometimes.

Utah is a beautiful and terrifying place.
You must drive through it.

You will find out what you need and what you cannot carry:
mockingbird, mourning dove, crow.

You are older than Jesus,
but not dead yet.

You feel claustrophobic
under smaller skies.

Possibility is a quicksand.
Home is a loose tooth.

You still can't tell by looking
if the tide is coming in or going out.

I'm Sorry I Haven't Sent the Letters I Promised

I wait for the needle after
the ultrasound's caress.

A towel under my neck tips
my head back on the exam table

my gaze fixed on a painting of a
forest so fluffy you could hug it.

The October ice storm hit
before the trees had lost their leaves

under the weight of such fortune
a jackpot of frozen green coins

the trees lost their limbs.
Back home Jane writes

*The few who have power
don't want people in their homes.*

In my dream last night the woman
whose heart I broke asked me for money.

The nurse offers me a shrug
I walk out into a gentle rain.

Here we are at the end of October,
already the Christmas trees are up at Target.

I miss dangerous weather.
It cannot be stopped.

I Never Told Anyone This Because It Just Happened This Morning

My dog discovered a sausage
discarded on the sidewalk.
An immaculate delicacy
that I tore from her teeth
and tossed away.
My dog, horrified,
placed her white paws
on the green compost bin
and prayed to her doggy gods
to resurrect the sausage from its tomb.

Once she unearthed an entire breast
of fried chicken from the bushes.
I took that from her too.
That was back in Oklahoma
where it is sunny all the time
and fried chicken is so prevalent
folks toss it out windows.

Here in Seattle
where all the food is raw
she barks at a crow enjoying
some rat sushi
dipping its beak
into the rodent's red gash.

This morning it is raining.
My dog refuses to go further
than the bushes to pee.
When she comes out
she's popping her jaws
like she's smacking gum
looking up at me with a guilty expression.

I reach into her mouth
to pull out whatever she's eating.
I'm holding a man's yellowed molar.

I shriek and toss it away.
The tooth ricochets against the building.

I wipe my hands in the wet grass.
Tell myself that this never happened
It wasn't a tooth.
It was just weird bone.
I haven't looked in a mirror in days.

Riding the Ferris Wheel at the Beginning of the Apocalypse

Seattle, Washington, March 11, 2020

I am almost at the end of being young.
We are almost to the end of the world
or it feels like that
at the end of the pier
at the end of winter.

There are no lines, the carnival is empty.
Bored workers take our tickets.
No one drinks the beer and wine they sell.

The ride is too gentle.
I want the carriage to rock a little
just for the thrill of it
so I can feel what is happening.

I can't decide which way to face.
Toward the lights of the city
and all the people who are sick but unaware?
Or out over the darkness of Puget Sound?
The black water seems more solid than liquid—
leather or wrinkling skin.

I turn away to take a photo
of the crooked line
where the light meets the dark
my own face reflected on the glass.

The ride lasts longer than promised
five revolutions instead of three
before coming to an end.

If this is the end let them not say
I should not have wandered
so far from home
to spend the end like this
untethered in a city searching
for colored lights and a little joy.

If this is the end the pictures came out blurry.

Opera Man Serenades Us on a Pandemic Date

A crowd gathers around a gray-haired man
presiding from his porch.
We find a spot on the grass
sit close but not touching.
Around us families pull toddlers in wagons
small dogs yip, wag their tails.
One woman's tote bag drips red wine
onto the street, into the grass
a ritual offering.

In a jean jacket and rumpled chinos
Opera Man is a rooster ready to crow.
He launches into song
a sad clown lamenting fate
bewailing the wiles of women.
Sirens howl in the distance
a baffled UPS driver negotiates the crowded street
children cry, dads suck on bottles of beer.

When Opera Man arrives triumphant
at his finale, "Nessun dorma,"
I'm so drunk with joy
sunshine and possibility
it doesn't seem right
to be this happy.

Aren't we all just sad clowns
trying to get through this?
Death and grief prowling the yard
around our healthy bodies.
Bodies soaking up the sun, the music
eager to be moved, to be touched
all of us hungry for pleasure
to finally find joy within our reach

to learn how to live
here so close to the end.

This evening the light is so long
it seems it could last forever.
It will not.
Neither will the night.

A Brief History of Information

I am a librarian who rarely touches books.
It's not my job anymore.
I look through a computer
to help others use a computer.
After I do that, I look at my phone
caress it with my thumbs
scroll through status updates
pictures, profiles,
looking for a laugh
or love or doom.

Scroll used to mean
a piece of parchment rolled up
then unrolled whenever the king
wanted to behead his wife
or announce his betrothal.

There were a lot of scrolls
in the Library of Alexandria
(and why it was so flammable).
I read on Facebook that it was forbidden
to read silently to one's self.
If you wanted to read a scroll
you had to read aloud in a booming voice
so that everyone around you could hear.
Silent reading was considered selfish,
sneaky, a sign of nefarious purposes.

It must have been a very loud place.
A discordant chorus,
like my library after story time
or before the Republican
Women's breakfast meeting.

Or at least it was, pre-pandemic.
Now it's very quiet
while we sit at the reference desk
and wait for the phone to ring.
Steve and I blast
Wagner's *Götterdämmerung*
one Saturday morning, because, why not?
We're the only ones listening.

In the Middle Ages books were chained
to the library shelves, guarded by monks.
In Jim Crow, only whites allowed,
information, a tool of hate.
A library is defined by those who use it.

Sometimes I fall asleep and dream
in Dewey Decimal
811 American poetry,
709 Art and artists, historical,
614.57 Plague,
020 Library and information science.

Fernweh *Is the Cure for* Heimweh

Take everything you have
divide it into three piles:
Everything you will give away.
Everything you will throw away.
Everything you will keep.
Wind will take it all
and give it back to you broken
into something new.

Leave for the home of wind.
Your restless flesh believes
your restless home awaits.

Wind is feral, it snaps and bites
refuses to be held but it holds you
runs its fingers through your hair.

Carry wind's shape.
Appoint yourself heir
beloved daughter of wind
she who wanders not to be lost.
Become accustomed to leaving and arriving.
Pick things up to put them down.
Make walls shake. Feel at rest
only in empty spaces. After all
who are you
without something missing?

Home is the sound of howling.
Sing this song.

My Ex-Girlfriend, Oklahoma

Dear Oklahoma,
By the time you read this I'll be gone six months
and you'll just be getting out of lock up
for your second DUI.
Listen, I'm sorry, but
you are a bad girlfriend
you keep breaking my heart
and embarrassing me in public.

I won't be sending any checks
but I'll write you poems
about the way you make me sweat
the way you sing like locusts
devouring a field
the way you flash your thunderheads
and promise me a tornado.

I love your big oily heart
the way it fracks
the way it wails
on Saturday night at the Blue Door
when you call yourself Freedom
say you're from Bartlesville
when you're really from Sayre.
I love the way you wrap your legs
around the closest girl to your barstool
and lick her up the back of her neck.

Sunday morning you roll into church
a little bit late and a lot hung over
and never say nothing
about loving the sinner.

Everyone knows the best way to end things
is to get her name tattooed on your body
but I never got that scissor-tailed flycatcher
to fly across my shoulders.

My new lover
(who's never even been to a Walmart)
asks me
Do you miss your home?
I don't know what to say so I point up
and say *I miss the sky.*

Maybe it's the sky
I need marked across my body
the emptiness I love
in a shape I can touch.
Maybe I don't need wings anymore.
Maybe I need an anchor.
Maybe I need a whole flock of birds
perched on a telephone wire against the setting sun.
Maybe a pumpjack, a dust bowl,
the deed to some mineral rights,
Oral Robert's praying hands.
Maybe I need wind, hail, flash floods, and ice
a whole cycle of storms rotating across my body
to get over my grief about walking away from you
your crimes and your prayers
your crumbling textbooks.

I thought I could be a stranger.
I thought I could fill my pockets
with rattlesnakes
fistfight with the dust
every glancing blow a farewell.

Oklahoma, you're trash.
I'm trash, too, for leaving.
I've gone broke
trying to bail you out.
I can't fix you
but this won't ever be over.
No one needs me like you.

The Poem I Need to Write

Will have horses
wild ones.
No one can touch them.
But you will ride them around the pond at midnight.
The poem I need to write is a scuffed boot
a flashlight, a circus leaving town
only sawdust remaining.
The poem I need to write is a sign
off the highway in Henryetta, Oklahoma.
It reads *Hungry Traveler Restaurant.*
No restaurant to be found.
The poem I need to write plays Erik Satie
on a rubber chicken, drinks
the last glass of wine in the bottle.
The poem I need to write is the amplified
spooling of desire, hooves beating
outrunning the bite of sorrow
speeding toward horizon.
The poem I need to write has equal parts
bliss and nonsense running in its veins,
knows what it is like to lose your vision.
The poem I need to write is rain falling
through sunshine. Purple storm clouds
in the distance. Red mud tracks
on your white carpet. It is a living season.
The poem I need to write says
it is a long way home in the dark.
It will never be enough.

The Sky Responds to My Entreaties

after Holly Wilson's *Guardian and Guide*

I give you one foot for flying
one foot on the earth
keep stepping forward
even when precarious
movement is a balancing force

creating equilibrium
you must learn to hang
in the unfinished web
to spin you must learn
when to hold on

when to let go
when to let the wind
sweep it all away
to disappear and start over
allow beauty to enter

along with everything else
you must weave your own web
trust the silk when it arrives
know that it takes time
cannot be forced

the secret is in your grip
not too tight
but all your energy
look at the shadows
that move with you

meet the clouds halfway
I release you
blank is the end
blank is the beginning

an empty-handed leap

NOTES

"Tennessee Williams Speaks to Joe Exotic about the Southern Gothic" was inspired by the Netflix documentary, *Tiger King*.

"Work: A Ghazal for Oklahoma" was written in response to the botched execution of Clayton Lockett by the state of Oklahoma on April 29, 2014.

"Tulsa 1998": The center of the universe is a small circle of concrete inside a larger circle of bricks. If you stand at the center of the circle, your voice will echo, but the echo will be inaudible to those outside the circle. The center of universe is located in downtown Tulsa on a pedestrian railroad overpass along Boston Ave. between 1st and Archer Streets. This acoustical vortex was created by accident in the 1980s when the bridge was rebuilt after a fire.

"The Land We Belong To": Then Governor Mary Fallin declared October 13, 2016, as Oilfield Prayer Day in response to falling gas prices. The proclamation states, "People of all faiths are invited to thank God for the blessings created by oil and natural gas industry and to seek His wisdom and ask for protection."

"Graciela Says" was inspired by reading *Photographic: The Life of Graciela Iturbide* by Isabel Quintero and Zeke Peña, published in 2018.

"Postcards": *Heimweh* is the German word for "homesickness," or literally "home-sore." The opposite of *Heimweh* is *Fernweh*, often translated as "wanderlust," the ache to visit faraway places.

"Opera Man Serenades Us on a Pandemic Date": Stephen Wall, a tenor from the Seattle Opera, gave free weekly short concerts from his front porch in the Ballard neighborhood of Seattle, beginning in April 2020 until September 2021.

"The Poem I Need to Write" was inspired by reading Barbara Ras's book of poetry *Bite Every Sorrow* (1998).

ACKNOWLEDGMENTS

Many thanks to Jane Vincent Taylor and Jeanne Castle, who read many early versions of these poems and provided so much helpful feedback and support. Where I would I be without the both of you? Thanks to all of my friends at Ghost Ranch for the joy of writing together. Thanks to my teachers at Hugo House, especially Judith Skillman, who taught me how to assemble a manuscript. Thank you to my parents, who instilled in me a love of reading and libraries. Thank you to Emma Harrison (and Molly and Maggie) for your love and all our adventures together.

Many thanks to the editors of the following publications where these poems first appeared, sometimes in different versions:

All Roads Will Lead You Home: "About the Chicken," "Foreman of the Detasseling Crew"

Anti-Heroin Chic: "Boundless," "My Ex-Girlfriend, Oklahoma"

From Sac: "Notes on Sky-Watching," "The Sky Responds to My Entreaties"

Lavender Review: "June Valentine"

Mockingheart Review: "The Poem I Need to Write"

Open Minds Quarterly: "Long Lost"

Plainsong: "Elizabeth Bishop Reads My Horoscope"

Poets House Community Anthology: "Coming Out in Oklahoma"

Right Hand Pointing: "Last Day of 37"

San Pedro River Review: "The Next-to-Last Lesbian Bar in Oklahoma City"

Screen Door Review: "Tennessee Williams Speaks to Joe Exotic about the Southern Gothic," "Symptoms of Escape Fever Include," "Elizabeth Bishop Swipes Right"

Shark Reef: "Books, Boots, and the Blank Page"

SWWIM: "Scripture of the Fireflies"

This Land: "Work: A Ghazal for Oklahoma"

Whale Road Review: "On Why You Should Change Your Life Every Seven Years"

SERIES ACKNOWLEDGMENTS

We at Wheelbarrow Books have many people to thank without whom *Landlocked* would never be in your hands. We begin by thanking all those writers who submitted manuscripts to the twelfth Wheelbarrow Books Prize for Poetry. We want to single out the finalists, Mary Ardery, Rebekah Hewett, Jenny Manthey, and Liz Marlow, whose manuscripts moved and delighted us and which we passed onto the competition judge, Thomas Lynch, for his final selection.

Our thanks to Kelsey Block, Laura Horan, Cindy Hunter Morgan, Natalie Mannino, and Estee Schlenner for their careful reading of manuscripts and insightful commentary on their selections, and especially to Laurie Hollinger, assistant director at the RCAH Center for Poetry, who also read the manuscripts and provided the logistical aid and financial wizardry for this project.

Then we go on to thank Stephen Esquith, former dean of the Residential College in the Arts and Humanities, who gave his initial support to the Center for Poetry and Wheelbarrow Books, and current dean, Dylan Miner. Conversation with June Youatt, former provost at Michigan State University, was encouraging, and MSU Press director Gabriel Dotto and assistant director Julie Loehr were eager to support the efforts of poets to continue reaching an eager audience. Thanks also to Lauren Russell, director of the RCAH Center for Poetry, for her support of Wheelbarrow Books. We cannot thank all of you enough for having the faith in us, and the love of literature, to collaborate on this project.

Thanks to our current Editorial Board, Sarah Bagby, Gabrielle Calvocoressi, Leila Chatti, Carol V. Davis, Mark Doty, George Ellenbogen, Carolyn Forche, George Ella Lyon, Thomas Lynch, and Naomi Shihab Nye for believing Wheelbarrow Books was a worthy undertaking and lending their support and their time to our success.

Finally, to our patrons: without your belief in the Wheelbarrow Books Series and your generous financial backing, we would still be sitting around the conference table adding up our loose change. You are making it possible for poets, when publishing a new volume of poetry is becoming harder and harder these days with so many presses discontinuing their publishing of poetry, to find an outlet for their work. As well, you are supporting the efforts of established poets to continue to reach a large and grateful audience. We name you here with great admiration and appreciation:

Beth Alexander	Fred Kraft
Gayle Davis	Jean Kreuger
Mary Hayden	Brain Teppen
Patricia and Robert Miller	

There are many others whose smaller contributions we value whether those contributions come in terms of dollars, support for our programming, or promoting the books we have published and the writers we treasure. Thank you, one and all.

WHEELBARROW BOOKS

Anita Skeen, *Series Editor*

Sarah Bagby   George Ellenbogen

Gabrielle Calvocoressi   Carolyn Forché

Leila Chatti   Thomas Lynch

Carol V. Davis   Naomi Shihab Nye

Mark Doty   George Ella Lyon

Wheelbarrow Books, established in 2016, is an imprint of the RCAH Center for Poetry at Michigan State University, published and distributed by MSU Press. The biannual Wheelbarrow Books Poetry Prize is awarded every year to one emerging poet who has not yet published a first book and to one established poet.

SERIES EDITOR: Anita Skeen, professor in the Residential College in the Arts and Humanities (RCAH) at Michigan State University, founder and past director of the RCAH Center for Poetry, director of the Creative Arts Festival at Ghost Ranch, and director of the Fall Writing Festival.

The RCAH Center for Poetry opened in the fall of 2007 to encourage the reading, writing, and discussion of poetry and to create an awareness of the place and power of poetry in our everyday lives. We think about this in a number of ways, including through readings, performances, community outreach, and workshops. We believe that poetry is and should be fun, accessible, and meaningful. We are building a poetry community in the Greater Lansing area and beyond. Our undertaking of the Wheelbarrow Books Poetry Series is one of the gestures we make to aid in connecting good writers and eager readers beyond our regional boundaries. Information about the RCAH Center for Poetry at MSU can be found at http://poetry.rcah.msu.edu and also at https://centerforpoetry.wordpress.com and on Facebook and Twitter (@CenterForPoetry).

The mission of the Residential College in the Arts and Humanities at Michigan State University is to weave together the passion, imagination, humor, and candor of the arts and humanities to promote individual well-being and the common good. Students, faculty, and community partners in the arts and humanities have the power to focus critical attention on the public issues we face and the opportunities we have to resolve them. The arts and humanities not only give us the pleasure of living in the moment but also the wisdom to make sound judgments and good choices.

The mission, then, is to see things as they are, to hear things as others may, to tell these stories as they should be told, and to contribute to the making of a better world. The Residential College in the Arts and Humanities is built on four cornerstones: world history, art and culture, ethics, and engaged learning. Together they define an open-minded public space within which students, faculty, staff, and community partners can explore today's common problems and create shared moral visions of the future. Discover more about the Residential College in the Arts and Humanities at Michigan State at http://rcah.msu.edu.